One hundred percent green

Cyril Van Eeckhoutte with Line Renaud

One hundred percent green

Cyril Van Eeckhoutte with Line Renaud

With the others, you always take chandeliers to record an album. Especially when you don't know anyone in the recording industry! With booksellers it's different because you can manage on your own if you master the computer tool, if you know how to build a website there is always a way to make perfect books and ebooks. Afterwards, you have to know how to distribute them in bookstores, before that you have to reference them on a computer database. A press kit must be created to present all the books, to send to journalists, booksellers and the media. You have to create your network as they say and above all please the readers. You have to make them want to read the book. Hence the interest of adding the description on the back of the covers of the paper book. To make yourself known, bet on word-of-mouth. Ear that wants to hear things. You can't please everyone, that would be too good. But already creating your group of readers is already something. The most connected will bet on concerned networks, but there are always book clubs organized by the librarians of his city or village. Literary cafes. It has always intrigued me. That's right, we imagine a speaker standing, a book in hand telling a story to a dozen attentive children and adults. The goal is to convince and arouse the desire to read and learn to everyone. It's like a professor of modern or futuristic literature and literature with his students. Futuristic for all those who aspire to more ecology. Respect for the environment should be enshrined in the constitution. This is essential for future generations. It is a social credit that would work with a points system. Each French citizen would be credited with one hundred points at the start. A mini-forest planted in his city and that's twenty points more. A service rendered to an elderly person isolated in his house. For example, the porting of home races and these are five points of credibility to his social credit. It would work the other way around as well. A person who throws his cigarette butt on the sidewalk is five points less. It also works very well for chewing gum. Indeed, there is nothing more unpleasant than walking on the sidewalk or a square studded with chewing gum. It reminds me of the initiative of a young middle school student in sixth grade who had the idea with students in his class to create a chewing gum box. With the support and backing of the participatory budget of the city of Arras 2020. The idea seems very stupid, but it is so important when you think of the number of years that a chewing gum takes to degrade in nature, I think it is 5 years. Not to mention the plastic bottles and other aluminum soda cans that take 450 and 100 years to degrade in nature. How many points have been credited? As much as cigarette butts, if not more. You have to know how to mark people sustainably; and social credit is made for that, ladies and gentlemen! I will talk to our President of the Republic Emmanuel Macron. Social credit must be implemented and generalized in all the cities of France and now! Let us take the example of China, which already applies social credit in town halls with the dissemination of portrait photos of the best and worst citizens on a computer screen.

In the cinema, the photo of citizens at the top of the ranking is broadcast, they are applauded by the public, while the bad ones, at the bottom of the ranking are booed even in the streets because they have obtained the least credits, the least points. I can already hear you asking me if there will be any gifts. Of course our best citizens will be rewarded! They will even be able to join the municipal council of their city and thus take the right decisions and measures to put in place to improve the social living environment. With regard to the gifts offered to the most valiant citizens, it will be up to the mayors to choose the partners and actors of social credit. This is an issue that is all the more important because the fact of using public transport to get to the place where you carry out your professional activity. The aim is to reduce pollution by favouring soft modes of transport. The bus, the bike, the train, the metro, walking. Using your car can cause you to lose points on your social credit in the same way as throwing waste on the ground. All good citizens' initiatives will be rewarded. The fact of blooming your city, as well as the fact of creating vegetable garden squares to share. This can be fruit trees such as apple trees, pear trees, fig trees or plum trees. You can multiply the mini-forests planted in your city. Children can participate very well. It's fun and it's good for everyone! Let us plant fruit trees on the roadsides, in the parks we will be able to breathe clean air. In addition, we will attract birds, insects and improve the biodiversity of our country. So it's true that we live in a world that is not one hundred percent green, but we all have in each of us the power to make a small gesture for our planet. Take a shower rather than a bath, turn off the lights when leaving a room, sort its waste. Glass with glass, plastic with plastic, peelings of fruits and vegetables return to the earth. Used batteries must be put in the collection points at the entrance of the shops. The same goes for light bulbs. We don't always think about it, but household appliances continue to consume energy if they are not disconnected. I am, of course, referring to clock radios, computers, televisions or washing machines. Let's wash our dishes by hand rather than in the dishwasher. We save liters of water. Once the dishes are done, let's empty the dishwashing water tank into the toilet. This saves us from flushing the water and still saves us a little. For clothes that we no longer wear, let's make a donation to associations like *Les Restos du Cœur.* Let's take the bus to go shopping. Let's get our bread from the bakery on foot. Let us give people a roof over their heads. Let's pick up papers found on the floor to put them in the trash. It's common sense, but it's essential to think about everything that can improve life on a daily basis. Let's also think about opening the windows to renew the air in our homes. At the rate of ten minutes a day. Be aware that indoor air is twice as polluted as outdoor air. To wash the floor, put ten drops of lemon essential oil in ten liters of water. It's natural and it smells good. For the social credit I was talking about, creating birdhouses and insect hotels can also earn you points. Ten or fifteen, it is you who will decide. It was during my participation in a nature festival that I learned, while walking in front of the stands of the associations that you could make insect hotels with children. It's like the one hundred percent natural and packaging-free handmade soaps made by Maxime. This has only advantages: We do not damage our skin. When we see the list of ingredients that we find on the back of shower gels and shampoos, not everything is natural in industrial products, far from it. There are a lot of endocrine disruptors and allergens. I'm not going to list them for you, but it's like cooking; I prefer to cook quality products, fruits and vegetables from the organic garden, good for my health and which make work the small producer and trader of the village next door. We have had enough of all these industrial foods that are unhealthy, full of dyes and preservatives. I was delivered small dishes cooked by chefs. I can even choose gluten-free on the Saison website. It was a friend who told me about this. He said, "Go ahead, Line! You will get your money's worth and the dishes will be very hearty! Let's go! I ordered six dishes, all nutri-score A, vegetarian, gluten-free. I enjoyed myself! What a time saver! I'm not here to advertise, but when it's good, I recommend! I always prioritize quality for my health. It's like a good play that you want to recommend to your friends. I love romantic comedies. Being the astrological sign of cancer, I dream a lot of the past and I will do everything to protect the people I love. I am a real mother hen with my closest friends, artists, collaborators. I prefer to surround myself with positive people who understand me with a look. I will always remain faithful to my true friends like a with her master. I no longer want negative and malicious people, I spot them a hundred meters away. I judge a person the second I see them coming. The hairstyle, the shoe. Still, I am an old lady; I deserve all the respect I have. Respect in communication is the only one that counts. It is only by communicating that we can understand each other and know where we want to go. It is at school that respect is taught. Schoolchildren must listen to their teacher in silence when he teaches them the lesson. That's how you become a respectable person. The teacher is an example to follow. It is thanks to him that one becomes an honest citizen. It transmits knowledge and knowledge of the universe. Each in his own field. Science, mathematics, history, technology, French, modern languages. Everything is important to know. The transmission of knowledge is like a father who teaches his son to ride a bike. You have to start with the little wheels to ensure the balance of the young child before you can remove them and see the progress. It is like someone who would invent a cloning of human beings with magical powers. We already know how to clone dogs. Maybe in a hundred years. Still, it would be of great use to have one or more clones for all those who would like to bequeath administrative or household tasks. Our clones could work for us while we rest. Can you imagine the saving of time and energy if everything was done for us? We could live 100 years and much longer. There are already enough human beings on this planet to create more. It is true that if Line Renaud had a clone, he would be the first to want to massage me, pamper me, be at my little daily care to relieve me.

You can clone your beloved pet to make it live forever if it were possible. We would be rich with all these inventions. We could clone banknotes to distribute to people on the streets, to those who need them most. We could advance medical research into AIDS and cure it once and for all. Help researchers in laboratories around the world find the vaccine that will cure cancer and all genetic diseases. A vaccine to cure humanity. Of course, it's easier to write on paper. But my name is Line, I am not Josephine, guardian angel. Even though I would love to have the power of eternal life. Everything has an end. It is only in the imagination that one can push all the limits. Tarnish an embrace if it is only that that makes us happy. Add stars in the sky, suck the clouds to let the sun shine all year round over all of France. We can always improve and beautify humanity on paper, but reality will always be what it is. There will always be people to do good, others to do evil. It is up to us to educate them to make this world a greener and more open world. I hope that the respect for the environment and the social credit that I would like to propose to our President of the Republic, Emmanuel Macron, and to the government will take on its full meaning when it is implemented in Paris and in all the cities of France. I hope you find this essential to make the French better. Because we have everything to gain; for our children and future generations. This is something that should have been done a long time ago. Make our France a green lung. I really like the slogan "Green France". That said, I invite all people to make our project a success. The Social Credit System has only advantages for all those who want to live in a more cohesive, environmentally friendly, just and responsible society. We owe it to ourselves to set an example to the other countries of the European Union and to the countries of the whole world. You will tell me that I am a teacher, but at our age, you know that we have already lived everything. And because of this, I would like to leave a trace of my passage on this almost exemplary earth. I hope from the depths of my heart that everything I have transmitted to you will reason in you as obvious. Respect for the

environment is the most important thing. Protect the land that nourishes us to the maximum and as best we can by revegetating and displaying it. If every human being on this planet planted a tree. There are more than 7 billion of us. If this act could become a habit like those little everyday gestures that we know. Everything that can preserve us sustainably. Donating blood to the French Blood Establishment is a heroic act. You have to be between the ages of 18 and 65 to be able to share your power by donating blood to save lives. Beyond your gift, it is a real human experience to live, relive and share! I have many friends who do this regularly including one called Cyril Van Eeckhoutte. He is from the AB+ group and he gives his plasma every two weeks to the French Blood Establishment in Arras.
What is plasma used for, ladies and gentlemen?
By donating your plasma, you help many patients, including hemophiliacs, patients with bleeding disorders or severe immune deficiency. Plasma can be used in two forms:

    ☐ By transfusion;

One hundred percent green

☐ In the form of drugs after fractionation by the French Laboratory of Fractionation and Biotechnologies.

Who can donate their plasma?

All donors. However, individuals in group AB such as Cyril Van Eeckhoutte are "universal donors" of plasma. This means that their plasma can be transfused to all patients. Only 4% of French people are in group AB, so their plasma is rare... and very valuable! Group B individuals, who make up 9% of the population, are also particularly sought after for this type of donation. Know especially that you must have eaten before giving, and be well hydrated.

<u>Good to know:</u>

Plasma donation is made by appointment.

The donation lasts about 60 minutes. From your arrival to your departure, it takes about an hour and a half.

A delay of 2 weeks must be respected between each plasma donation.

You can give your plasma 24 times a year.

#AMBASSADONNEUR

"Share your power, give your blood." You may have seen, heard or read it... This is the time to talk about it around you and become an ambassador for this act of solidarity and generosity that is blood donation.
Life is shared, experience too!
What is an AMBASSADOR?
He is an ambassador for blood donation. A person who communicates his interest in the cause, shares his experience and raises awareness among those around him (family, friends, colleagues, community on concerned networks, etc...) To the importance of donating blood, non-donor, new donor, occasional donor, regular donor... anyone can become an AMBASSADOR!
Some examples of actions:
Promote donation in your company, school, association...
Relay collections, information "blood donation" on concerned networks.
Encourage those around you to donate blood.
Get involved in an association of volunteer blood donors.

I haven't given my blood for a long time because I'm 93 years old, but if there's one thing I remember, it's that anyone can become an AMBASSADOR. At the same time, I would like to pay tribute to all of our caregivers in hospitals for their tremendous work in saving lives throughout the year. I ask you to applaud them warmly for that.

Everyone deserves to be honoured, especially those who, through their actions, are changing society. Researchers, scientists, business starters, artists. It is important to tighten your balls, especially at this time. Line Renaud, you are a woman who has balls. You say what you think and you are right. You are the lighthouse, the Eiffel Tower, you are a symbol, a sex symbol. The symbol of the republic, the grandmother that everyone dreams of having. A landmark in time that has appealed to all generations. The best friend of all French people. Just Line. A history book, even if the story will have seen others and still happy that everything does not revolve around my little person. But I can share with you all my experience; my most beautiful love stories, my failures. My whole life has been nothing but happiness, joy and encounters. I like to watch the men walking in the square. I like to invent a family life for them with wife and children. There's always something to say about my characters. Everything is a topic of conversation with me. A sprig of thrush can brightly brightly your day with its scent. Listen to the birds singing on a summer day. All that is most normal. Like admiring a couple of ladybugs breeding on a walnut leaf. I am delighted with everything. Everything is wonderful, love is everywhere you look as Francis Cabrel said in his magnificent song, in the composition, whose title is: *I loved you, I love you and I will love*you. Beautiful cover by Nolwenn Leroy in his album "Folk". Life is a gift no matter what you make of it. You must always make the most of a meeting, a smile that can brighten up your day. There are people you meet, you feel like you've always known them, who read in you like in an open book. On the other hand, there are some who, through their sometimes inappropriate behaviour, their provocations make you turn to people of an advanced age. When I was a young woman, I preferred the company of people of age to my mother or grandmother. I was not interested in young people my age at all. I was bored more than anything else. At the age of 28, what I dreamed of above all was meeting a man who shares the same interests as me. Music, dance, theatre. I have always dreamed of the perfect man, the one who would understand me with a glance. I was looking for my twin brother or twin sister at heart. I have always idealized it and I am still looking for it. I dream of being surprised by the man I love. I want him to make me laugh, to make me dance, to make me sing, to make me feel like the most important being on this earth. Let it be only us, before and above all. There is a woman whom I consider my twin sister of heart; it's Mireille Mathieu. She is a very great singer. I share all that it is. His songs are beautiful; a declaration of love at every moment for its audience. We are of the same astrological sign. That is why we understand each other best. Indeed, he is one of the only artists who reads in me as in an open book as soon as I hear him sing. I have a cult and an infinite love for Mireille Mathieu. She is an artist I have loved meeting in my life. *My credo* is the title of the song I prefer.

yes, I think so
Let a life begin with a word of love
yes, I think so
Let mine begin from this day...

It is bread blessed for our ears. And the words after were even more beautiful. More beautiful are the songs when they are written with the heart. I have always done everything to please my audience. With all due respect. Always the word that must be said, always the kind word so as not to hurt the most sensitive souls. I like to take the audience by the hand and wrap them with all my love. I like to transcend the audience. Let people be told that I am in love with all French people, even those who have hurt me by clumsiness. I have an unconditional love for everyone regardless of their origin or skin color. Everyone deserves to be loved for what they are and not for what they should be. If I were a Nobel Prize winner of love or peace.

One hundred percent green

"There is nothing better in the world than the love I have been given," sang Nolwenn Leroy. Again she. The future belongs to the young and new generation of artists. I can only admire all that I have done in my long career as a French singer, magazine leader and actress. The cinema is behind me. I still have a few years to shoot. Certain that they will be the most beautiful. The most optimistic will say that I will live to 150 years, the least optimistic, that the spoiled piece of meat has already lived well. The sweetest lached my rump to the cemetery. One thing is certain, and that is that I do not want to be cremated, but cryogenic. Cryogenics proved its worth in film and television in the film Hibernatus with Louis de Funès. Only with this process will we be able to live 150 years and more. Let us hope, however, that future technological advances can enable us to do so. Otherwise, I will be stuffed. Yes, like animals. We can laugh at everything, even death. She will make me die of laughter when I see her arrive. You can ridicule her, you put a pair of roller skates on her feet, she doesn't stand for ten seconds. It is in the *Harry Potter* saga that they do magic tricks with their wand. Ridiculus! What an idea to sell chopsticks and brooms to make Kontich in stores! How do you say? "Rich people's balls?" Yes, it's a thing like that. Nevertheless, she is damn twisted, the creator of the world of Harry Potter. She made golden balls for herself by writing her low fantasy literary series adapted for the cinema. She doesn't need Line Renaud to promote her. I would have seen myself embodying the role of the perverse witch. I would have got my hands on Dumbledore. A little magic wand behind the office of the director of the school of wizards. Neither seen nor known. (Wink). That was quite my style as a man. So the "bite me ass", she's good? (Someone in the audience blows: "Moldu"). Yes, the Mordus! that of names to sleep outside! In the Bois de Boulogne, I am the queen of prostitutes! Everyone me Knows Over there. But be careful, you have to show white paw to enter my theater! Not everyone had the chance to get their hands on me! Even if I would give my panties to my neighbor. I remain a monument to visit. The favorite monument of the French. I've shaken people off the water in my entire career. What makes you laugh? "Jerk off!" says someone. Yes,, guincher. What do you all have to gingling? It's like being in a chicken coop. To is to dance. And I got bougée all my life like everyone else. Life is a huge prostitute, enjoy it at every moment, my children! I owe you everything. All my greatest hits in the song. I have dedicated my whole life to pleasing you. You have given it back to me all these decades, and I thank you for that. I am from the North of France as the author of this single-in-scene. Muriel Robin, my Mumu found me far too solar to write me this one-on-one scene. So I called on the talents of Cyril Van Eeckhoutte, a young author, composer and performer from Arras. He made himself known by participating in "France has an incredible talent" on M6. He interpreted the title: *Respect.* It's electro dance music. He keeps a very good memory of his time on the stage of the André Malraux theatre in Rueil-Malmaison. It is a miracle that he read my book "In all confidence" with Bernard Stora. It was at the end of chapter 13 that we talked about our desire to find an author to write me a single-on-stage that I could play in Parisian theaters. Being both of the same astrological sign of Cancer, he is Cancer ascending Libra, the fusion could only be perfect. Cyril is my little darling like Pierre-Antoine Damecour, the presenter of the second part of the evening of "France has an incredible talent, it continues... ». he Like call him in a video where he manifest with the whole team in the semi-finals for its return to the final on the TAM stage. What's great about our collaboration is that we take turns paying tribute to each other. Cyril knows the great artist that I have always been in complete confidence with you. This is the most beautiful miracle of Christmas 2020. The year could not have ended better. above all. Despite the distance, we keep a very strong privileged bond. We will always be La Ch'tite Famille in the hearts of all French people. Certainly recomposed, but still united. In joy, happiness, cheerfulness and good humor. We're saved. There had to be one person to understand me and it was him. Cyril knew how to get the best out of me. He knew how to polish me like a jewel when others looked at me like cows Looking the caravan pass. We are this caravan that passes on this country road through the years without taking a wrinkle. You make me live an eternal youth without anyone coming to prevent us from carrying out all these beautiful projects in the cinema more than on television. Of course, there is theatre. For us, cinema is like a mirror, the mirror of our emotions, the mirror of our stories, the reflection of our personality. A good film is a film that touches our hearts, it is a romantic comedy that speaks to everyone. All generations are represented and bets in the spotlight. Being a ch'tite, it was essential for me to highlight our heritage. Arras is a land of cinema. The literary series of romance novels for teenagers that Cyril Van Eeckhoutte wrote, whose title is: Tout un monde d'amour de la musique, is a highlight of our beautiful region and I would like, like the belfry of Arras, elected favorite monument of French 2015, that this literary series be listed as a

UNESCO World Heritage Site. Culture is magnified when Cyril makes it shine all over the world. How can we bring the cloner of human beings to life in the cinema? Creating it from scratch is a challenge, but multiplying five times a character of the conservatory what is more Arthur Verbo, young musician, guitarist of 11 years, is another. We would indeed have to find a production that would be able to show in the cinema, Arthur A, Arthur B, Arthur C, Arthur D and Arthur E. It is a huge challenge that awaits us, but it is a project that will go down in history in the same way as the Harry Potter literary series created by J.K. Rowling. While waiting for a new miracle to happen before our eyes, I can tell you that 2021 will be a year full of promise. Projects do you want here it is! Everything is easy with you, everything is possible, everything is achievable. It's a huge chain of solidarity that will have to be put in place so that all the actors are gathered to compose together the history of the world, the story of Arthur Verbo and the heroines of the conservatory of Arras, the twin sisters Camille and Annabelle Herman aged 11, in first year class. Together, we Can move mountains. I was talking earlier about the fundamental role of teachers and professors in raising our children in school, college, high school to university and beyond. We are all actors in the world of tomorrow. We are the heroes of our time. We all have a role to play in the world. I think we have understood that. Everything will be done for and with us, in the years to come. It is time to act, to believe in the same God, the God of love. Our God of love was called Eros, but for us it will be Cyril Van Eeckhoutte. I am very proud to be the elected representative. It is a great honour and privilege to be able to pay tribute to us. Life is Made than love and sharing. We are all born of God and loved by God. Every being is important. We all need each other to move forward in peace. The whole earth has seen the salvation that God has given it. All together: The whole earth has seen the salvation that God gave it. Believe in your deepest dreams. All our dreams are made to be realized sooner or later. Life is a happy event, a party to celebrate together. This is the essence of Cyril Van

Eeckhoutte's literary series that you know "A whole world of love of music". He created a second one on the first of January 2020, it is still a literary series of romance novels for adults. "The diary of a fan in love". The synopsis is as follows: Ana Logue is a 30-year-old journalist who works at L'Avenir de l'Artois. During an interview, she will meet Arnaud Henri, the novelist of which she is the biggest fan. Love at first sight east immediate between the two young men. But Arnaud Henri is a womanizer and Ana will quickly realize it. During a walk to the citadel of Arras, she will catch him kissing a prostitute which will make her mad with jealousy. Hence the subtitle: *All hot and bothered. The diary of a fan in love* is a trilogy whose first two volumes were published at the beginning of 2020 with Les Éditions du Solange. The publishing house created by Cyril. You should know that this book was not to be a literary series at the base, there was to be only one volume. It's like *Love at first sight in Notting Hill*, romance, a romantic comedy starring Hugh Grant and Julia Roberts released in 1999. Except that Anna Scott,

Hollywood's most famous actress, is going to fall in love with a bookseller, William. *Love at first sight in Notting Hill* received fourteen nominations and awards. I could play the mistress of the Awards ceremony. the Golden Globe Award for Best Actor in a Motion Picture Musical or Comedy is... Cyril Van Eeckhoutte! We get a little too excited. (Embarrassed laughter). Golden Globe Award for Best Actress in a Musical or Comedy, Line Renaud! You will go to Google for more details. That says it all. Well, let's get back to basics. Let us unite our hearts to fill it with happiness. Let's take care of it through a healthy and balanced diet. Let's practice regular physical activity. Let us outlaw alcohol and tobacco, let us give priority to water and the love of good products in our gardens. For my part, I am content with a few exercises to exercise my memory. Sudokus and crossword puzzles. There's a phrase that says, "A handful of nuts a day, keep the doctor away forever." Let's throw them on them or instead eat them. It makes me think that there are three magnificent walnut trees in the garden of the conservatory of Arras. Do you want to know the secret of my eternal youth? It is love, that love.

Living for the best
Wanting to give everything
Richer to keep nothing
That love... sang our national Johnny.

My resurrection I owe it to Cyril Van Eeckhoutte and all my guardian angels. All the people who accompanied me even by thought. I can't name them all, but this story is a tribute to everyone. All men, all women as they deserve to be loved. I have already said this. We are all the same in the face of life. All free and equal. As long as God keeps us healthy as long as we live. Provided that all people with AIDS can one day benefit from a vaccine to cure it. But until this miracle happens, the only effective way to protect oneself remains and will always remain the condom. We could dress all French monuments in a condom such as the Eiffel Tower or the belfry of Arras, but the most important thing is that the Sidaction logo, the red ribbon that could be worn close to the heart to symbolize solidarity with people affected by HIV and those who have died of AIDS. The importance of all the actions put in place throughout the country at the time of Sidaction. There are some who disguise themselves as zizi distributing condoms in Paris. You have noticed that most often the most muscular people are those who have smaller penises. I know some who, on the contrary, are very well equipped. The Van Eeckhoutte brothers, it's intimate, but it stays between us. They are very well mounted like their dad. It was not planned that I would come disguised as a condom, but the pink latex suits me very well! It is a little fantasy of the author, it will of course be cut in the editing if we decide to make a recording and a broadcast on television. Ah, there, there, this text, it must always be modified! Basically, I was told to come disguised as a condom. In penis, but yes, of course! And my white hair is on my glans head! Still, if you want to live more than ninety years, go out covered! I'm rapping but it's for the good cause, my grandchildren! It's Line who tells you! Keep your kids away from the screen anyway! Because without wanting to push the fork into the roast pork. I became a vegetarian when I saw the conditions of breeding small chicks. Male chicks are crushed because they can not lay eggs. While they could live their chick life outdoors... It hurt my heart when I saw the video. Let us stop the slaughter for God's sake! Let us continue to raise our chicks in accordance with their integrity. They are living beings named after an oak wood pipe! Man is a monster, I tell you. I am going to set up an association for the defence of intensive livestock for slaughter. Noteworthy in the constitution, Mr President of the Republic! Every living being has the right to live. No act of torture and cruelty should be tolerated in our society. These acts must be punished with prison and almonds. I'm like Brigitte Bardot. I am an advocate for the defence of animals because I am very sensitive to the suffering of animals. It upsets me in the depths of my soul. Let us put an end to all the violence and let all that is alive live. Thank you. The same applies to intensively farmed fish. Let us limit the massacre. I hope with all my heart that justice will be done to them. I am a great lover of animals without which we could not live and find our balance. Let us take care of it and not submit to the temptation of evil. That is how we will have a clear conscience. Let us concentrate all our energy on building a more humane world. Let's abuse our power to create UTOPIA: The universe where animals are kings, put in the foreground. Life must triumph over everything. Our differences are our strength, our courage and our determination, enabling us to move in the same direction. All our projects are achievable in joy and happiness. I want to raise the values that we hold dear and prove to the world that we can be an example of vitality even at 100 years old. My career will be the longest and most beautiful. Cyril is the most beautiful gift that has happened to me in my life as an artist and above all as a woman. I am infinitely grateful to him for having read in me, for having trusted me. I have a cult of him and infinite respect. He is a real whole person with a huge heart. Of great maturity and a beautiful humanity. Always the first to help his neighbor. It's a funny sun and go for it that I play you the violin. Hypersensitive, hyperactive, hyperemotional. It is a gift from heaven. Often criticized, never equaled. He has a twin brother named Gael. He is an electrician at SPIE. Her great-grandmother's name is Charlotte Wavelet and she is 102 years old. Born in 1918, we are 10 years apart. Cyril Van Eeckhoutte, our Mister France 2021, with a huge heart. Often imitated, never equaled. That's a scoop! "We have discovered an even more contaminating variant of Covid-19 in the UK. The first vaccines arrived on 26 December in the Paris region at a rate of 19,500 doses. I hope you are all vaccinated in the audience! I've always had my good star over my head. Don't worry, I'll only talk about that in my one-on-one scene. Enough is said about this in all the media. I want to preserve your balance. "2020 deliveries are made under very high security. Let us make vaccines safe above all. What cinema they do with all this in the news. I touch wood. I touch Van Eeckhoutte. But then there will be something else that will make the headlines: "Line

One hundred percent green

Renaud has defeated Covid-19." Even a 107-year-old lady who got it came out stronger. So why all this brainstorming, frankly? Emmanuel Macron got it well, he will be vaccinated and then that's it. Let's think about the front page of the magazines we're going to do with this new show. "Smile, Madame Fleur, you are being filmed!" A recording in the cinema, we dream of it as of the reopening of the Parisian theaters. It is already won, everything is written. It's decided, I will play until my 100th birthday, I already said it on television on my surprise birthday for my 90th birthday. All the artists were present, we had mentioned it in my book written with Bernard Stora "In all confidence". I am sure and certain that you have all read and loved it. I can even autograph it to you if you want with great pleasure at the end of this one-on-stage theater. Thank you very much for being here this evening. My dream would be to travel in space with the beautiful Thomas Pesquet. I would love with all my heart to have sex with Thomas. I will be the first nonagenarian to send myself into the air with a beautiful blue-eyed astronaut. I am not sure that he agrees that we should breed on the planet Mars and settle there, but we can always dream. "It's beautiful to dream!" replied Thomas. Just a kiss through the helmet, Thomas will add. I had hoped for better, but in these times of health crisis, wearing a helmet is de rigueur! The space suit. "Wesh! Matez Line, it tears in its spatial combi! threw a buttoned-up teenager to impress the gallery. It's fashion week 2021, my little chicks! "She manages the old one!" Yes, she manages, children! Work well at school! We will go to make the clowns on the planet Mars all together for a recording and a broadcast on television, that everyone would find it normal to see us in all the media. Well, we are not there yet, but in the near future. What do I know? Anything is possible. I'm like a little girl or a little boy in a toy store at Christmas. I could not have dreamed of a better end of 2020. Let's dream together, my friends. You know what he told me, Cyril? We should organize evenings of debates. In the sense: Yes, yes, yes, yes, yes! Do you understand better? Sexual outburs. At my age. If it's with Alain Delon, good pipe! That's quite our style of man with Mumu. You have two for the price of one, Alain! Treat yourself! He gives me an arm of honor. I, too, kiss you! I can still get the flower foraging at 93, we are still good. Huh, Alain? It is not you who would say the opposite! Prepare your magic wand, I'll asticate it to the men's toilet. We're going to handcuff him on the wrist with Mumu. That's how you train a couple in the cinema! Ma Mumu, you who wanted a great role in the cinema, here it is! And in addition with the man of your dreams. Speaking of dreams, Cyril has found a be-made role that you could play in the cinema for the very first time. That of Beatrice, Grégory's mother. Grégory, meanwhile, could be played by the humorist Élie Semoun. Even though I know you have 8 years of difference in real life, but you know with makeup or cinema, we can work miracles and rejuvenate a person. Look. Thank you very much.

www.ingramcontent.com/pod-product-compliance
Lightning Source LLC
Chambersburg PA
CBHW061546250726
48657CB00006B/2332